Curses and Blessings

Other Books by Bradley Trevor Greive

Curses
and Blessings
for All Occasions

Bradley Trevor Greive

**Andrews McMeel
Publishing, LLC**
Kansas City • Sydney • London

Andrews McMeel Publishing, LLC
an Andrews McMeel Universal company
1130 Walnut Street, Kansas City, Missouri 64106

www.andrewsmcmeel.com

12 13 14 15 16 TEN 10 9 8 7 6 5 4 3 2 1

ISBN: 978-1-4494-1484-9

Library of Congress Control Number: 2011944673

Attention: Schools and Businesses

Andrews McMeel books are available at quantity discounts with bulk purchase
for educational, business, or sales promotional use. For information, please e-mail the
Andrews McMeel Publishing Special Sales Department: specialsales@amuniversal.com

Introduction

When it was brought to my attention that the global population had surpassed seven billion, I suddenly realized there were far more people I might need to insult than I had initially thought. Being a tight-panted optimist, I assumed there must be at least one or two extra praiseworthy souls, as well. Therefore, not wanting to slide back into the unctuous inarticulate mass, it seemed prudent to brace and hone my tongue for the snubs and meritorious moments to come, for these shall undoubtedly be legion. Thus, my gift to you, dear reader, is this delicate yet deadly volume of carefully crafted comic curses and blessings for all occasions.

If, like me, you have ever found yourself at a loss for words when things have gone horribly wrong, or been left speechless when an outcome exceeded your wildest expectations, then this little book may well be your salvation. Don't ever let another pivotal human encounter be compromised by a cerebral sputter, leaving you slack-jawed and foolish. Now, no good deed shall go unheralded: no slight is too small for a premium verbal skewering.

With my personal pocket library of potent and pithy utterances—designed to be deployed every day, with devastating effect—you can effortlessly smite your enemies and, when warranted, massage a friend's tender buttocks with a sweet and buttery verbal balm.

Having carefully tested these curses and blessings on animals, aristocrats, and common folk (as well as politicians and other lesser beings), I guarantee that these tastefully caustic quips will brighten up otherwise forgettable exchanges with people whose triumphs and foibles matter more to you than they probably should.

BTG

May your dancing shoes be filled with helium.

May breath mints prove futile.

May your corpse be museum worthy.

May all dairy items
in your fridge
be of
questionable
vintage.

Ooooooh . . . So bloated.

May a blinding epiphany
burn a gap in your unibrow.

Your skin is, like, so dry. Have you tried guacamole? I know—weird, right? But last summer my best friend got sunburned while we were in Cancun, and I found this guacamole in our minibar fridge, so I put it on her face and shoulders, and she looked, like, so amazing! She still had hideous strap marks, which looked so gross, so I made her wear a poncho to dinner. Have you ever been to Cancun? It's, like, so amazing, and the Mexican language is, like, so beautiful. . . .

May your masseuse be chatty.

May your incisors be parsley resistant.

May your swimsuit be snug.

May you be able
to read in bed
by the light of your soul.

May small dogs exploit your insecurities.

May your French kissing be awarded three Michelin stars.

May your tubes of toothpaste and hemorrhoid cream
appear identical in poor light.

Is that a hoagie in your pocket, or are you just glad to see me?

May your pockets be deep enough
to smuggle baguettes.

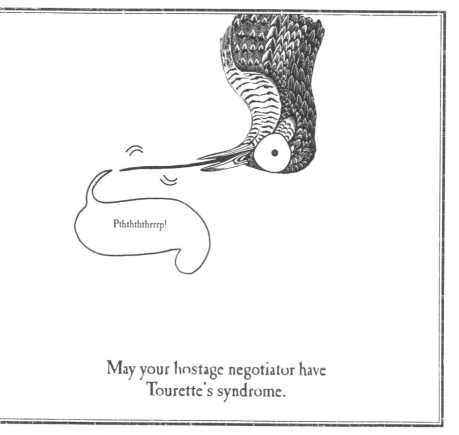

May your hostage negotiator have
Tourette's syndrome.

May your gait be ungainly.

May your lunch box not contain Schrödinger's cat.

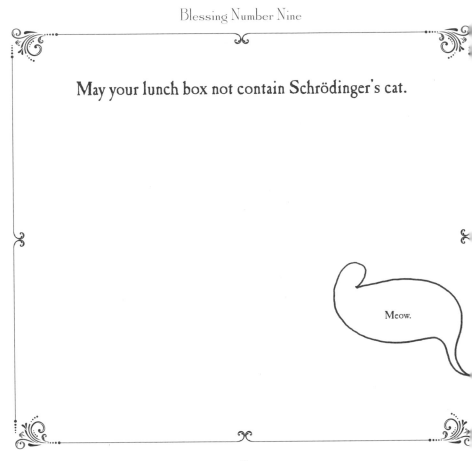

Meow.

May your stunt double develop osteoporosis.

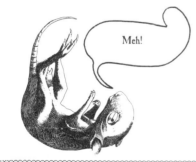

May cats acknowledge you.

May you possess an astonishing volume of
unremarkable underwear.

May your yogurt be teeming with bacteria.

May your court-ordered anger-management counselor be a mime.

May the jazz gods give you foxy fingers.

Oh yeah!

May a pineapple become lodged in your urethra.

May your neighbor's rooster have a sore throat.

May licentious shrimp spawn in your tartar sauce.

May you be the recipient of a sweaty man hug.

May your blocked pores be licked clean by angels.

May you lose a testicle at a cockfight.

May your loins firm up
at precisely
the right moment
to ensure your
place in history.

May Lady Justice
harden the hands
of your gynecologist.

May venerated
scholars
violently disagree
as to the
true merits
of your life.

May your nipples
attract inordinate
attention in church.

May your singing cause pandas to ovulate.

May the soundtrack of your life feature spooky flute music.

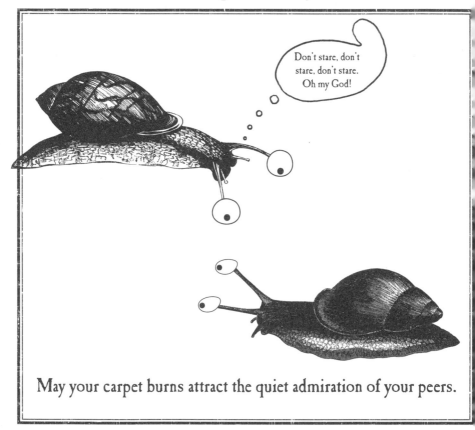

May a bomber formation of incontinent geese
fly over your sunroof.

May a Brazilian blowout change your life.

May a spider crawl out of every jar you open.

Alas, I am what I eat!

May your blood turn to gazpacho
in the presence of vegan vampires.

May faith healers revive your soufflé.

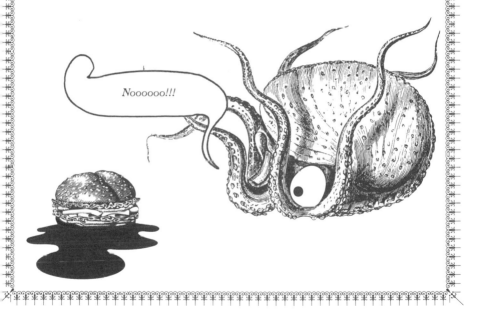

May beetroot bleed through your salad sandwich.

May your winter wardrobe make you look chunky.

May frostbite
claim your
supernumerary
nipple.

May low-cut jeans allow your merkin to escape.

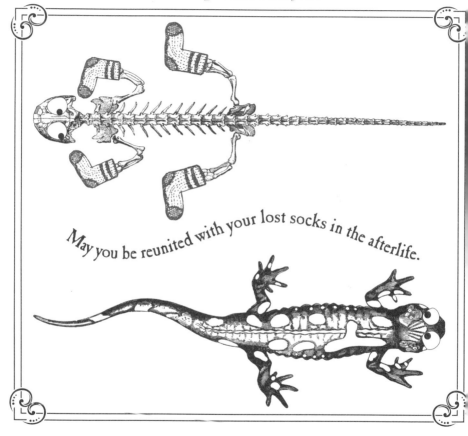

May you be reunited with your lost socks in the afterlife.

May your life begin and end with diaper rash.

May your G-Spot glow in the dark.

May reality
television
dissolve the
boundary
between
your psyche
and your
rational self.

May your libido exceed that of
a thousand unwashed goats.

May a frigid hedgehog
seek refuge
in your codpiece.

May your deodorant

not be found wanting

in the face of your

impending doom.

May you invest in a duplex with inadequate soundproofing.

May your excuses for avoiding tedious social engagements always sound credible.

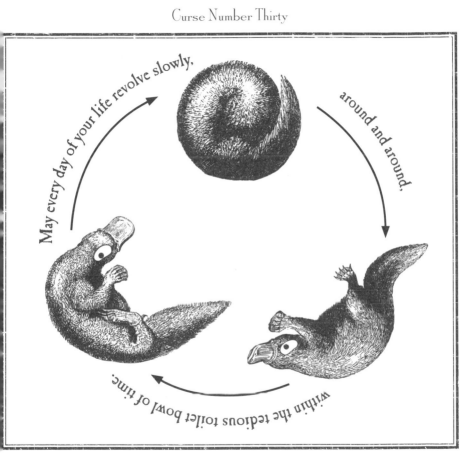

May every day of your life revolve slowly, around and around, within the tedious toilet bowl of time.

May your tears erase wrinkles.

May the source of your curious carpet odor be unclear.

May your flatulence be carbon neutral.

May you be devoured
by a single ant.

Amy Melin

Since the debut of his international best-seller *The Blue Day Book*, Bradley Trevor Greive has sold more than 22 million books in 115 countries. He is currently one of the most successful humor authors on the planet, and thus is largely responsible for the decline of the English language. A former Australian paratrooper, BTG left the army to seek creative misadventure. He has been bitten by wild monkeys and rabid bats and was accepted into Russia's cosmonaut training program, though these incidents were, by and large, unrelated. BTG was born in Hobart, Tasmania; however, his present whereabouts are unknown.

To find out more about the happily dysfunctional creative world of BTG, visit www.thelostbear.com, and to enjoy BTG's free cartoon features, go to www.gocomics.com/the-lost-bear.